WITH TABLATURE

GUNS N' ROSES
APPETITE FOR DESTRUCTION

CONTENTS

Management: Stravinski Brothers/Alan Niven
Transcribed by Jesse Gress
Edited by Mark Phillips
Art Direction: Alisa Hill
Production Manager: Daniel Rosenbaum
Administration: Deborah Poletto

ISBN: 0-89524-386-5

APPETITE FOR DESTRUCTION is available on Geffen Records,
Cassettes and Compact Discs.

Introduction

Guns N' Roses emerged from the turbulent yet fertile L.A. club scene which was the spawning ground for Van Halen, Quiet Riot/Randy Rhoads, Motley Crue, Ratt and Poison. Beginning with a small local undergound following, they rapidly garnered a greater public awareness with their raw no-nonsense sound and energetic rock 'n' roll feel. Their appearance and subsequent popularity in 1987 was concurrent with a perceptible shift in audience taste towards more direct and more emotional forms of rock — a reaction against the slick over-calculated pop/rock and the technically demanding metal fusion of the early and mid 80's. In this regard, Guns N' Roses advocate and deliver a musical presence which is the very essence of rock — rebellious, immediate and evocative. The music invites, indeed insists on, audience participation and involvement on a purely gut level.

The sound of *Appetite for Destruction* reveals an evolutionary link with the beginnings of modern rock. Sprinkled throughout the Guns N' Roses offerings are allusions to well-established and unmistakable '60's blues roots. The vocabulary of the blues/rock tradition of the British dynasty of the Yardbirds, Cream and Led Zeppelin is apparent in the guitar work of lead guitarist Slash, while the rough, aggressive rhythm work and powerhouse song riffs show the influence of the Kinks, early Stones and Aerosmith. These central elements coexist with hints of punk rock (in the pronounced chant-talk vocal approach of the verse in "It's So Easy" and the unabashed expletives found in the lyrics of "You're Crazy" and "Out Ta Get Me"), '60's psychedelic music (in the raveup jamming of the rideout outro solo of "Paradise City" and guitar-generated sound effects in the second guitar solo/interlude of "Welcome to the Jungle," in which stratospheric slide guitar adds a spacey quality to the proceedings) and vintage heavy metal (in the driving rhythm grooves, sustaining distorted guitar tones and visceral power chording throughout).

As in virtually all classic hard rock, the compositions of Guns N' Roses are essentially riff based. The riff, probably the most fundamental structural component in rock songwriting, is generally constructed from a strong repeating thematic unit which succeeds in grabbing the listener with its accessibility and immediacy. In the music of Guns N' Roses, the riffs are well constructed — their compactness making them ideal for elaboration.

The guitar orchestrations and harmonizations are remarkable. Notice in "Rocket Queen" the melody-versus-rhythm counterlines in the intro, slide guitar timbres in the solo, and the numerous texture and dynamic settings employed — full forte ensemble, spacious arena-like guitar and rhythm accent accompaniment, and clean tone picked arpeggiated guitars. The harmonized guitar lines are often unpredictable and interesting, exploiting a number of interval relationships. Note the ambivalence between major and minor in the parallel harmony of "Welcome to the Jungle" as well as the variety of treatments applied to the intro riff of "My Michelle," from a light airy statement over quasi-rubato guitar chordal arpeggiations at mezzo forte to a loud metallic answer phrase (reminiscent of early Black Sabbath) harmonized in unison and then parallel thirds.

In discussing his personal guitar approach to the Guns N' Roses material, lead guitarist Slash admits to a preference for improvisation. Citing guitarists Jeff Beck, Jimmy Page, Eric Clapton, Pete Townshend, Joe Perry and Angus Young as primary influences, he feels an extemporaneous plan of attack lends more life and energy to the music. Slash generally tends to elaborate on and re-develop the solo content on stage, except for his "signature solos" (those moments which originally on record produced a definite recognizable thematic impression.) A definitive example of his lead guitar playing is the extended outro in "Paradise City." Here, he builds chorus upon chorus of relentless guitar improvisations over a fiery double-time rhythm feel. Starting with imitative paraphrasing of the vocal chorus melody he continually gathers momentum, finally reaching a high energy climax emphasizing fast riffing, various major and minor pentatonic, blues and diatonic combinations and sinewy string bending.

An important point offered by Slash was made in regard to compositional technique. The band writes together, pooling their collective resources and influences, resulting in a multi-faceted yet cohesive output. Bassist Duff "Rose" McKagan, for example, having previously played in a punk group, brought his influence to the tune "It's So Easy." Izzy Stradlin' (second guitarist) and Slash originally created the riff of "Mr. Brownstone" on acoustic guitars, and the timbre of wah wah electric guitar evolved later. The first draft of "You're Crazy" was initially played on acoustic guitar and at a much slower pace (almost a half- time shuffle) but evolved into the uptempo boogie-meets-punk groove captured on the LP. There is constant rethinking and experimentation at work within their arranging and composing framework.

For *Appetite for Destruction*, Slash recalled that he favored his "Gibson Les Paul and old Marshall half stack with a minimum of effects." Occasionally, a chorus unit was added sparingly to process cleaner guitar picking passages (as in the intro to "Paradise City") or a vintage Dean Markley talk box (which can be heard trading phrases with straight guitar in "Anything Goes') or a crybaby wah wah pedal was used (as in "Sweet Child O' Mine" and "Mr. Brownstone").

-Wolf Marshall

GUNS N' ROSES
APPETITE FOR DESTRUCTION

PERFORMANCE NOTES

Guns N' Roses' sound can be described as a cross between Led Zeppelin and early Alice Cooper, playing basic, straight-ahead rock with a flair for the bizarre. The guitar sound is primarily straight-jacked Gibson Les Pauls through Marshall amplifiers with little in the way of effects. Whether playing clean rhythm parts or maximum-crunch solos, the sound is raw and natural, as opposed to the untra-processed sound so many rock bands use today. The music comes out of early 70's blues/rock, relying on blues form alterations and established metal hooks, as well as some new twists of their own. Most of the guitar solos are based on pentatonic minor (1,b3,4,5,b7) and the blues scale (1,b3,4,b5,5,b7) as well as pentatonic major (1,2,3,5,6) and the major scale (1,2,3,4,5,6,7).

Welcome to the Jungle

This tune begins with muted picking, utilizing an echo device to simulate sixteenth notes. The tonality here is B minor; Gtr. I's riff is based on B pentatonic minor (B,D,E,F#,A), as is the soloing of Gtr. II. This gives way to the verse rhythm part based on A5; the soloing in the last bar of the intro is based on the A blues scale (A,C,D,Eb,E,G). The riff over E5 at the end of the verse is based on the E blues scale without the fifth (E,G,A,Bb,D).

The first guitar solo has an E7 tonality, as Gtr. I utilizes double stops made up of thirds, fifths and sevenths. The second half of the solo (bars 5-8) is reminiscent of Jimmy Page and is based on the E blues scale (E,G,A,Bb,B,D) with brief use of the major third (G#).

The bridge introduces a new tonality, D major, where the tune calms down a bit, before returning briefly to E7. This is followed by the second guitar solo, this time over C# minor and these lines are based on C# pentatonic minor (C#,E,F#,G#,B) for the first six bars, E Mixolydian (E,F#,G#,A,B,C#,D) for the next two bars, B pentatonic minor for two bars, E blues scale for two bars, and B pentatonic major (B,C#,D#,F#,G#) for two bars. This gives way to some ad lib sound effects with slide and echo, followed by a chromatic riff harmonized first by a minor third, then by a major third, eventually getting back to the chorus. (Listen closely to the recording to hear the different tones used by the rhythm guitars, which fatten up the sound.)

It's So Easy

The intro, verse and chorus sections of this tune are based on the E blues scale (E,G,A,Bb,B,D). After the intro, one guitar plays basic "5" chords, supported by a second guitar playing double stops. The bridge utilizes arpeggiated chords with open strings; allow all tones to ring as long as possible. This is followed by a rhythm part that is a variation on Rhy. Fig. 2, using a similar syncopation but different chords.

The guitar solo is also based on the E blues scale, primarily in 12th position. The attack is similar to Angus Young of AC/DC, featuring the sound on humbucking pickups with heavy picking.

The outro solo begins with phrases featuring "rakes," which means to strum with a single downpick sweep across muted strings, low to high. This solo is also based on the E blues scale, with momentary use of the sixth (C#) and the major third (G#).

Nightrain

The intro features two guitars, one playing single note lines, the other playing triads. The single note line is based on A Dorian (A,B,C,D,E,F#,G) until the G chord (bar eight), where the line is then based on G Major (G,A,B,C,D,E,F#), resolving to A5. The rhythm part for the verse sections is based on chunking chords with a muted line based on A pentatonic minor (A,C,D,E,G).

Fill 1 features some artificial harmonics (see tablature explanation page). Les Pauls and similar guitars with humbucking pickups are great for achieving these sounds (just ask Billy Gibbons of ZZ Top). The first five bars of the chorus rhythm part is reminiscent of the chorus rhythm part to Zeppelin's "Black Dog."

The guitar solo brings a shift in tonality to B minor, and the solo is based on B pentatonic minor (see "Jungle") for the first eight bars. The next section is based on two bars of D followed by two bars of F#5, which is repeated three times. D pentatonic major (D,E,F#,A,B) is used over F#5. The outro solo is based on A Dorian combined with the A blues scale (see "Jungle.")

Out Ta Get Me

This AC/DC-like tune begins with a G minor tonality, with the lead guitar using the G Dorian mode (G,A,Bb,C,D,E,F). The double stops in the solo are played by fretting both notes with the third finger. The guitar solo is based on the same scale and uses the same third finger technique. This solo is particularly reminiscent of Angus Young, with the fast, tight vibrato and hard pick attack. The second half of the solo is based on A pentatonic minor (see "Nightrain").

Mr. Brownstone

The return of the "Bo Diddley" beat, augmented by muted strumming on guitar with wah wah pedal. Follow the symbols to rock the pedal correctly. The descending riff by Gtr. I is not based on sounding precise pitches; just slide your finger slowly down the sixth string while picking sixteenth, and then slide back up. Rhy. Fig.1 is based on E Dorian (E,F#,G,A,B,C#,D) with a major third added (G#). The riff in bars 5-8 of the chorus is based on E pentatonic minor (E,G,A,B,D). The guitar solo features a shift in tonality to F#5, with the solo lines based on F# pentatonic minor (F#,A,B,C#,E). The sound is fattened up with wah wah pedal and echo. This is one of the more difficult solos, so work out the phrasings carefully. The second half of the solo is based on G pentatonic minor (G,Bb,C,D,F), C pentatonic minor (C,Eb,F,G,Bb) and D pentatonic minor (D,F,G,A,C) in the next three bars, respectively. All riffs are very similar and use the same basic hand positions and manipulations.

Paradise City

This tune begins like a country tune, arpeggiating first position chord forms. Use a combination of alternate picking and consecutive picking, whatever feels most comfortable. Riff B is based primarily on G pentatonic major (G,A,B,D,E). Again, the guitar is pusing a lot of distortion, sounding occasional artificial harmonics. Riff D is based on G pentatonic minor (G,Bb,C,D,F).

The guitar solo features the use of an octave divider which doubles all the notes one octave lower. The solo is based on G pentatonic minor for bars 1-4 and 7 & 8. Bars 5 & 6 are based on A pentatonic minor (A,C,D,E,G).

The double time section again features G pentatonic minor and G pentatonic major, and the solo guitar is played in the style of classic blues/rock, reminiscent of Lynyrd Skynyrd's "Free Bird" outro.

My Michelle

The best way to articulate the opening arpeggios is to hold each chord form through each beat and use alternate picking. Riff A is based on the F# blues scale (F#,A,B,C,C#,E), again emphasizing the b5(C). Riff B harmonizes Riff A a major third up. The four bar section before the guitar solo (after "...But till then ya better...") is based primarily on F# pentatonic minor (F#,A,B,C#,E); use the third finger to fret both notes in bar three. The following guitar solo is based primarily on B pentatonic minor (B,D,E,F#,A) with brief references to the G5 chord. Bar four and five of the coda recall rock 'n' roll rave-ups of old, especially Eddie Cochran's "Summertime Blues."

Think About You

The opening soloing lines here are like revved-up Chuck Berry, played in a tag team fashion by Gtrs. I & III. The rhythm part over the verse combines chord accents with muted root notes; play it so you can distinguish the two clearly, digging in to the part as a whole. W. Axl Rose sounds like Klaus Meine of the Scorpions on this tune. Rhy. Fig.1 and 1A complement each other well, power chords supported by arpeggiated triads; use a clean tone for the triads, crunch for the chords.

The guitar solo contains more Chuck Berryisms based on F# pentatonic minor (F#,A,B,C#,E). No flaming speed riffs here, just old fashioned rock 'n' roll.

The soloing at the end of this tune is based on B pentatonic minor (see "Michelle"), played in the standard pentatonic position.

Sweet Child O' Mine

Riff A is based on D Major (D,E,F#,G,A,B,C#) and is played on a Les Paul set on the rhythm pickup, with the tone turned way down. The groove is more laid back than most of the other tunes, kind of countryish and reminiscent of U2; the vocal part is reminiscent of Grand Funk Railroad.

The guitar solo section brings a change in tonality to E minor, and the solo lines are based on E Aeolian (E,F#,G,A,B,C,D), with brief reference to E harmonic minor (E,F#,G,A,B,C,D#). Bars 25-32 recall Alvin Lee's soloing on Ten Years After's classic "I'd Love To Change the World." The last part of the tune contains some fast soloing based primarily on E pentatonic minor (E,G,A,B,D); the quintuplet riff is actually a four-note phrase played as fast as possible, so the phrasing looks a little confusing. Listen to the record to determine how the guitarist is feeling the phrase against the beat.

You're Crazy

This tune sounds a little like AC/DC meets Bachman-Turner Overdrive on 78. Simple, straight-ahead rock 'n' roll played FAST. The eighth notes in the rhythm part should all be downpicked; this will definitely take some practice to get down. The chorus rhythm part is reminiscent of a San Francisco rock 'n' roll band of yesteryear, Rhinoceros.

The guitar solo is based on B pentatonic minor (B,D,E,F#,A). The riff in bars 9-12 is the same as what Jimmy Page plays at the end of his "Heartbreaker" solo. It may take some work to be able to hold the bend and apply a strong vibrato.

Anything Goes

For the intro, one guitar plays a little riff based on the chord tones of A7 (E,G,C#); this is a very common shape in rock, used by Jimi Hendrix in the opening to "Red House." The other guitar plays lines based on A pentatonic minor (A,C,D,E,G).

The guitar solo features a tonality change to E minor, with lines based on E pentatonic minor (E,G,A,B,D) with the inclusion of the sixth (C#) and E pentatonic major (E,F#,G#,B,C#). Working back and forth between these two scales is a common practice in rock, brought to the fore by Eric Clapton. Bars 5-8 feature the use of a "talkbox," a device which amplifies the guitar through a long, thin tube held in the guitarist's mouth, enabling him to shape the tone phonetically (similar to a wah wah pedal but to a much greater degree). The sound is then picked up by a microphone as if the guitarist were singing. The second half of the solo is based primarily on B pentatonic minor (B,D,E,F#,A).

The last section of the tune features a feel change to an uptempo shuffle, similar to but slightly faster than the Doors' "Roadhouse Blues." The last riff in the free section is based on the D blues scale (D,F,G,G#,A,C).

Rocket Queen

Riff A, as well as the ostinato soloing during the first verse, is based on F# pentatonic minor (F#,A,B,C#,E) with grace notes used from the minor third (A) to the major third (A#). Over the B5 and C#5 chord the lead guitar uses B pentatonic major (B,C#,D#,F#,G#) and C# pentatonic major (C#,D#,E#,G#,A#), respectively.

The slide guitar solo uses triad superimpositions primarily, much in the Jeff Beck style (as in the bridge of "Beck's Bolero").

The soloing during the outro is based on E pentatonic major (E,F#,G#,B,C#), which is the same as C# pentatonic minor starting from a different note (C#,E,F#,G#,B). Bars 13-15 utilize the E major scale (E,F#,G#,A,B,C#,D#), which is the same as C# Aeolian. Some tough phrasing here, so analyze the lines carefully and listen to the record.

-Andy Aledort

TABLATURE EXPLANATION

TABLATURE: A six-line staff that graphically represents the guitar fingerboard, with the top line indicating the highest sounding string (high E). By placing a number on the appropriate line, the string and fret of any note can be indicated. The number 0 represents an open string.

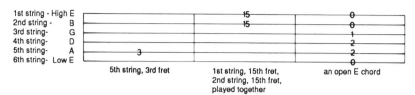

1st string - High E
2nd string - B
3rd string - G
4th string - D
5th string - A
6th string - Low E

5th string, 3rd fret   1st string, 15th fret, 2nd string, 15th fret, played together   an open E chord

Definitions for Special Guitar Notation

BEND: Strike the note and bend up ½ step (one fret).

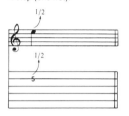

BEND: Strike the note and bend up a whole step (two frets).

BEND AND RELEASE: Strike the note and bend up ½ (or whole) step, then release the bend back to the original note. All three notes are tied, only the first note is struck.

PRE-BEND: Bend the note up ½ (or whole) step, then strike it.

PRE-BEND AND RELEASE: Bend the note up ½ (or whole) step. Strike it and release the bend back to the original note.

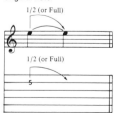

UNISON BEND: Strike the two notes simultaneously and bend the lower note up to the pitch of the higher.

VIBRATO: The string is vibrated by rapidly bending and releasing the note with the left hand or tremolo bar.

WIDE OR EXAGGERATED VIBRATO: The pitch is varied to a greater degree by vibrating with the left hand or tremolo bar.

SLIDE: Strike the first note and then slide the same left-hand finger up or down to the second note. The second note is not struck.

SLIDE: Same as above, except the second note is struck.

HAMMER-ON: Strike the first (lower) note, then sound the higher note with another finger by fretting it without picking.

PULL-OFF: Place both fingers on the notes to be sounded. Strike the first note and without picking, pull the finger off to sound the second (lower) note.

TRILL: Very rapidly alternate between the note indicated and the small note shown in parentheses by hammering on and pulling off.

TAPPING: Hammer ("tap") the fret indicated with the right-hand index or middle finger and pull off to the note fretted by the left hand.

PICK SLIDE: The edge of the pick is rubbed down the length of the string producing a scratchy sound.

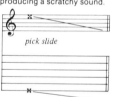

TREMOLO PICKING: The note is picked as rapidly and continuously as possible.

NATURAL HARMONIC: Strike the note while the left hand lightly touches the string over the fret indicated.

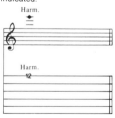

ARTIFICIAL HARMONIC: The note is fretted normally and a harmonic is produced by adding the edge of the thumb or the tip of the index finger of the right hand to the normal pick attack. High volume or distortion will allow for a greater variety of harmonics.

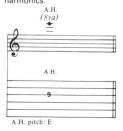

A.H. pitch: E

TREMOLO BAR: The pitch of the note or chord is dropped a specified number of steps then returned to the original pitch.

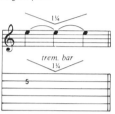

PALM MUTING: The note is partially muted by the right hand lightly touching the string(s) just before the bridge.

MUFFLED STRINGS: A percussive sound is produced by laying the left hand across the strings without depressing them and striking them with the right hand.

RHYTHM SLASHES: Strum chords in rhythm indicated. Use chord voicings found in the fingering diagrams at the top of the first page of the transcription.

RHYTHM SLASHES (SINGLE NOTES): Single notes can be indicated in rhythm slashes. The circled number above the note name indicates which string to play. When successive notes are played on the same string, only the fret numbers are given.

WELCOME TO THE JUNGLE

Words and Music by
W. Axl Rose, Slash,
Izzy Stradlin', Duff "Rose" McKagan
and Steven Adler

5

3rd Verse
w/Rhy. Figs. 1 & 1A

Wel - come to the jun - gle, it gets worse here ev - 'ry day.___ You

learn to live___ like an an - i - mal,___ in the jun - gle where we play.___ If you got a

hun - ger for what you see,___ you'll take it e - ven - tu'l - ly.___ You can have an - y - thing you want,___ but you
w/Rhy. Fig. 2

bet - ter not take it from me.___ In the jun - gle, wel - come to the jun - gle. Watch it bring you to your
(Ah, _____ ah.) ___

IT'S SO EASY

Words and Music by
W. Axl Rose, Slash,
Izzy Stradlin', Duff "Rose" McKagan,
Steven Adler and West Arkeen

1. I see your sis - ter in her Sun - day dress.__ She's out to please,__ she pouts

2.3. *See additional lyrics*

__ her best.__ She's out to take, no need__ to try.__ She's read - y to make.__

Additional Lyrics

2. Cars are crashin' every night.
   I drink 'n' drive, everything's in sight.
   I make the fire, but I miss the firefight.
   I hit the bull's-eye every night. *(To Chorus)*

3. Ya get nothin' for nothin', if that's what ya do.
   Turn around bitch, I got a use for you.
   Besides, you ain't got nothin' better to do,
   And I'm bored. *(To Chorus)*

NIGHTRAIN

Words and Music by
W. Axl Rose, Slash,
Izzy Stradlin', Duff "Rose" McKagan
and Steven Adler

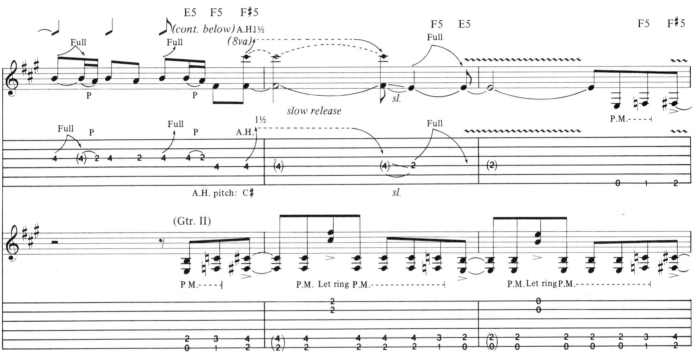

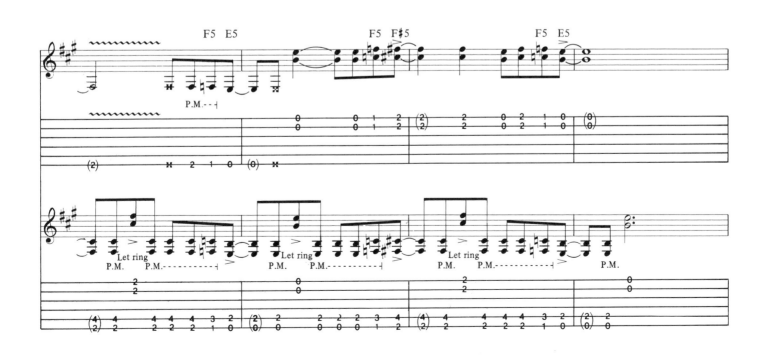

Additional Lyrics

Outro Chorus:
Nightrain, bottom's up.
I'm on the nightrain, fill my cup.
I'm on the nightrain, whoa yeah!

I'm on the nightrain, love that stuff.
I'm on the nightrain, and I can never get enough.
Ridin' the nightrain, I guess I,
I guess, I guess, I guess I never learn.

On the nightrain, float me home.
Oh, I'm on the nightrain.
Ridin' the nightrain, never to return.

Nightrain.

OUT TA GET ME

Words and Music by
W. Axl Rose, Slash,
Izzy Stradlin', Duff "Rose" McKagan
and Steven Adler

1. Been hid-in' out and lay-in' low. It's noth-ing new to me.
2. Some-times it's eas-y to for-get where you're go-in', some-times it's hard-er to leave.

Some peo-ple got a chip on their shoul-der, and some would say it was me.

MR. BROWNSTONE

Words and Music by
W. Axl Rose, Slash,
Izzy Stradlin', Duff "Rose" McKagan
and Steven Adler

Now I get up—a-round when-ev-er. I used to get up—on time. But

that old man,— he's a real muth-a-fuck-er, gon-na kick him on down the line.———

Coda II

Stuck it in the mid-dle and I shot it in the mid-dle and it,

it drove me out-ta my mind.___ I should've known bet-ter, said I wish I nev-er met her, said I,

I leave it all be-hind._____ Yow-sa!

Additional Lyrics

2. The show usually starts around seven.
   We go on stage around nine.
   Get on the bus around eleven,
   Sippin' a drink and feelin' fine. *(To Chorus)*

PARADISE CITY

Words and Music by
W. Axl Rose, Slash,
Izzy Stradlin', Duff "Rose" McKagan
and Steven Adler

1st, 2nd, 3rd, 4th Verses
w/Riff D (3rd, 4th times add Riff F)

1. Just a ur-chin liv-in' un-der the street.__ I'm a ____ hard case that's tough to beat.__ I'm your
2.3.4. *See additional lyrics*

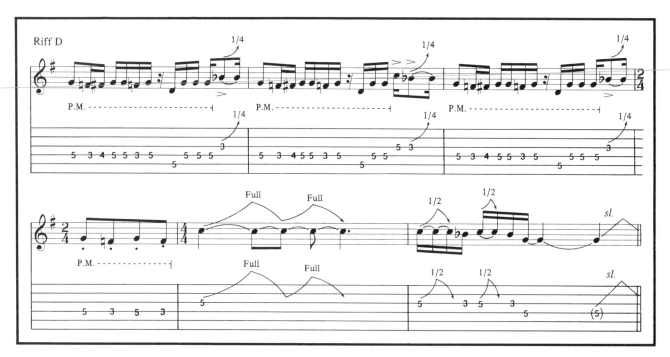

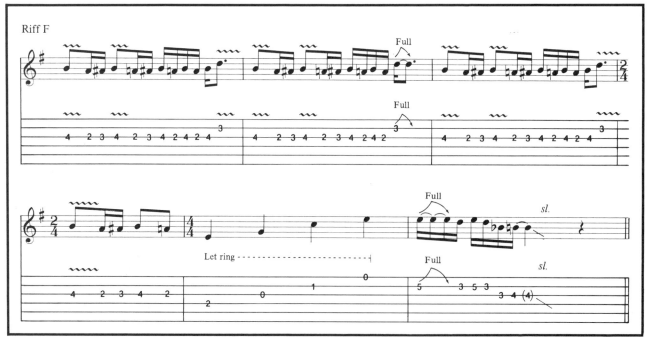

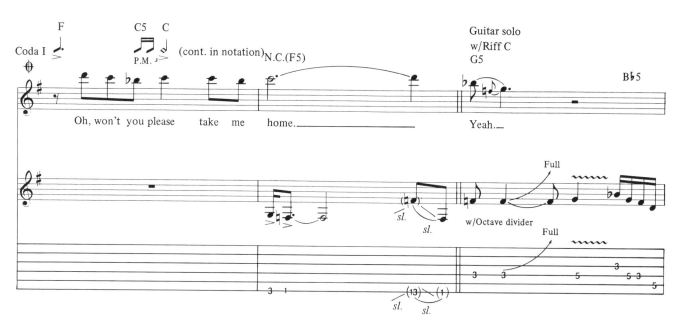

Oh, won't you please take me home._____ Yeah.__

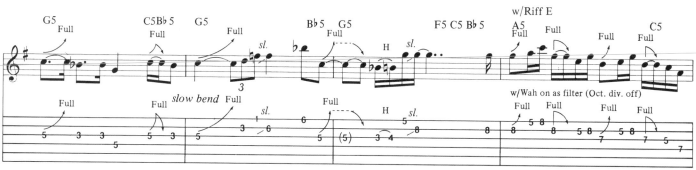

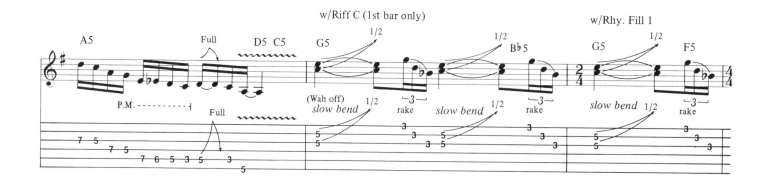

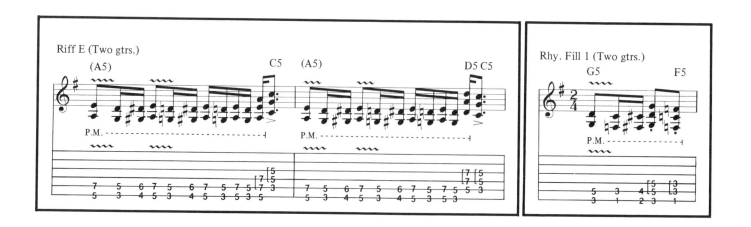

Oh, won't you please take me home,_____

home._____

* Slow slide up middle 4 strings (off neck)   *As before

Double time ♩ = 208

Rhy.
Fig. 3

(end Rhy. Fig. 3)

w/Lead vocal ad lib (on Chorus) *(till notation returns)*
*w/Rhy. Fig. 3 *(9½ times)*
**G5

w/Octave divider

*Vary strumming rhythm at will.
** Use "type 2" till end.

Additional Lyrics

2. Ragz to richez, or so they say.
   Ya gotta keep pushin' for the fortune and fame.
   It's all a gamble when it's just a game.
   Ya treat it like a capital crime.
   Everybody's doin' their time. *(To Chorus)*

3. Strapped in the chair of the city's gas chamber,
   Why I'm here I can't quite remember.
   The surgeon general says it's hazardous to breathe.
   I'd have another cigarette but I can't see.
   Tell me who ya gonna believe? *(To Chorus)*

4. Captain America's been torn a part.
   Now he's a court jester with a broken heart.
   He said, "Turn me around and take me back to the start."
   I must be losin' my mind. "Are you blind?"
   I've seen it all a million times. *(To Chorus)*

MY MICHELLE

Words and Music by
W. Axl Rose, Slash,
Izzy Stradlin', Duff "Rose" McKagan
and Steven Adler

1. Your dad-dy works in por-no now that mom-my's not a-round. She

2. 3. *See additional lyrics*

used to love her her-o-in but now she's un-der-ground. So you stay out late at night, and you

do your coke for free. Driv-in' your friends cra-zy with your life's in-san-i-ty.

Additional Lyrics

2. Sowin' all your wild oats in another's luxuries.
   Yesterday was Tuesday, maybe Thursday you can sleep.
   But school starts much too early, and this hotel wasn't free.
   So party till your connection calls; honey, I'll return the key.*(To Chorus)*

3. Now you're clean and so discreet. I won't say a word.
   But most of all, this song is true, case you haven't heard.
   So come on and stop your cryin', 'cause we both know money burns.
   Honey, don't stop tryin' and you'll get what you deserve.*(To Chorus)*

THINK ABOUT YOU

Words and Music by
W. Axl Rose, Slash,
Izzy Stradlin', Duff "Rose" McKagan
and Steven Adler

57

Additional Lyrics

2. There wasn't much in this heart of mine.
   There was a little left and babe, you found it.
   It's funny how I never felt so high,
   It's a feelin' that I know, I know I'll never forget.
   Ooh, it was the best time I can remember, *(etc.)*

3. Somethin' changed in this heart of mine,
   You know that I'm so glad that you showed me.
   Honey, now you're my best friend.
   I want to stay together till the very end.
   Ooh, it was the best time I can remember, *(etc.)*

SWEET CHILD O' MINE

Words and Music by
W. Axl Rose, Slash,
Izzy Stradlin', Duff "Rose" McKagan
and Steven Adler

Whoa, oh, oh, oh, sweet child o' mine.

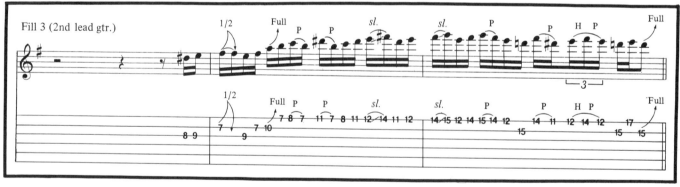

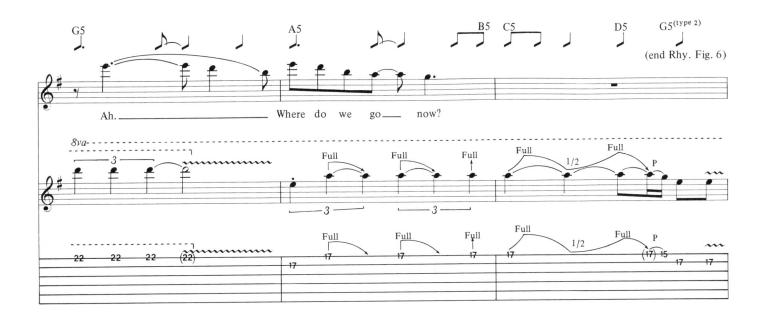

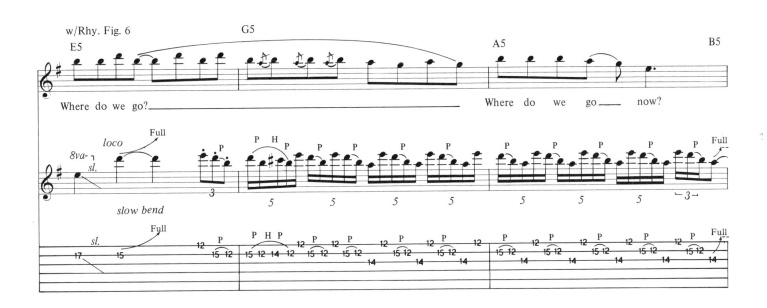

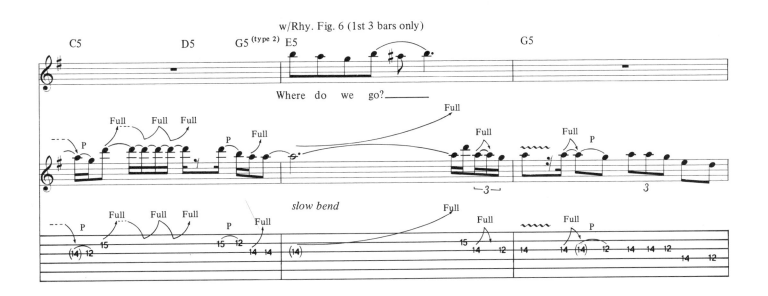

Additional Lyrics

2. She's got eyes of the bluest skies, as if they thought of rain.
I hate to look into those eyes and see an ounce of pain.
Her hair reminds me of a warm safe place where as a child I'd hide,
And pray for the thunder and the rain to quietly pass me by. *(To Chorus)*

YOU'RE CRAZY

Words and Music by
W. Axl Rose, Slash,
Izzy Stradlin', Duff "Rose" McKagan
and Steven Adler

*Both gtrs. bend

Additional Lyrics

2. Said where you goin'?
   What you gonna do?
   I been lookin' everywhere
   I been lookin' for you.
   You don't want my love, *(etc.)*

3. Say boy, where ya comin' from?
   Where'd ya get that point of view?
   When I was younger
   Said I knew someone like you.
   And they said you don't want my love, *(etc.)*

ANYTHING GOES

Words and Music by
W. Axl Rose, Slash,
Izzy Stradlin', Duff "Rose" McKagan,
Steven Adler and Chris Weber

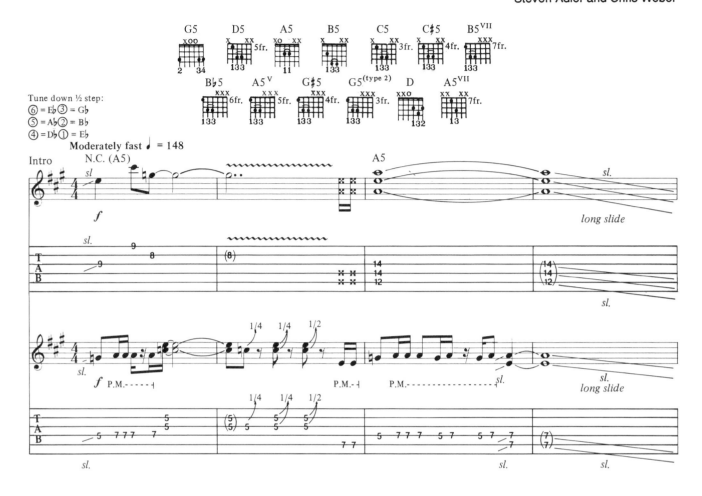

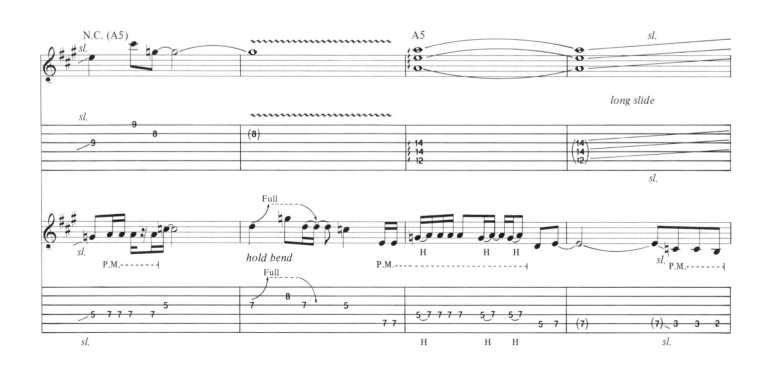

My way, your way, an-y-thing goes to-night,___

Fill 1

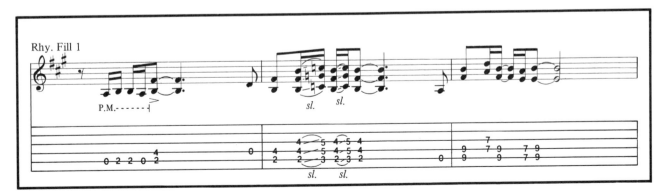

Rhy. Fill 1

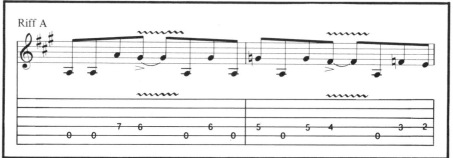

Additional Lyrics

2. Panties 'round your knees with your ass in debris,
   Doin' dat grind with a push and squeeze.
   Tied up, tied down, up against the wall.
   Be my rubbermade baby an' we can do it all. *(To Chorus)*

ROCKET QUEEN

Words and Music by
W. Axl Rose, Slash,
Izzy Stradlin', Duff "Rose" McKagan
and Steven Adler

*Slide bar off neck and back.

Riff A1

Riff B

Riff C

Play 3 times

Here I am,—

Learn with the BEST

EDDIE VAN HALEN

STEVE VAI

JIMMY PAGE

JOE SATRIANI

JIMI HENDRIX

NIRVANA

ERIC CLAPTON

STEVIE RAY VAUGHAN

METALLICA

GUNS N' ROSES

PEARL JAM

NUNO BETTENCOURT

ERIC JOHNSON

GEORGE LYNCH

KEITH RICHARDS

JEFF BECK

AC/DC

Become a better guitarist and performer—
Study with the professionals every month in GUITAR.

Just **$22.95** buys you a year's subscription to *GUITAR* and the chance to spend
12 Months studying the techniques and artistry of the world's best guitarists.

Every issue of *GUITAR* gives you:
- Sheet music you can't get anywhere else, with note-for-note transcriptions of the original recordings.
- In-depth interviews with guitar greats who candidly discuss the details of what they do — and how they do it.
- Columns and articles on the music, techniques, and equipment that are essential for today's guitar player.

GET STARTED NOW!
Call or write to save nearly 52% off the cover price!

303-678-0439

GUITAR Magazine
P.O. Box 1490 Port Chester, NY 10573